The Gruesome Truth About

The Vikings

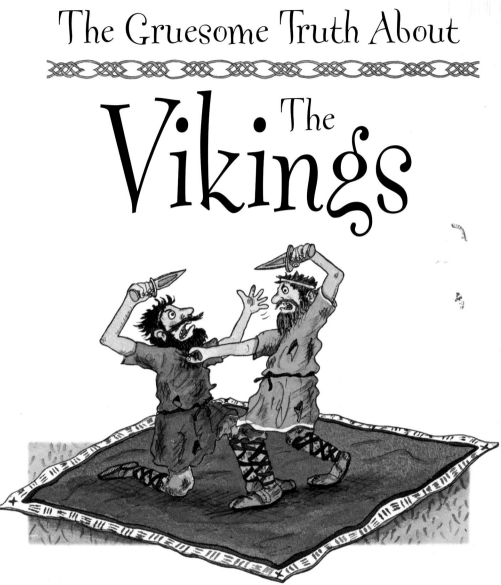

Written by

Jillian Powell

Illustrated by

Matt Buckingham

First published in paperback in 2012 by Wayland

Wayland
338 Euston Road
London NW1 3BH

Wayland Australia
Level 17/207 Kent Street
Sydney NSW 2000

Editor: Victoria Brooker
Designer: Jason Billin
Consultant: Martyn Whittock

British Library Cataloguing in Publication Data
Powell, Jillian
The gruesome truth about the Vikings
1. Vikings--Social life and customs--Juvenile literature.
2. Civilization, Viking--Juvenile literature.
I. Title II. Vikings
948'.022-dc22

ISBN 978 0 7502 7095 3

Printed in China

First published in 2010 by Wayland
Text copyright © Wayland 2010
Illustration copyright © Matt Buckingham 2010

Wayland is a division of Hachette Children's Books,
an Hachette UK company.
www.hachette.co.uk

Contents

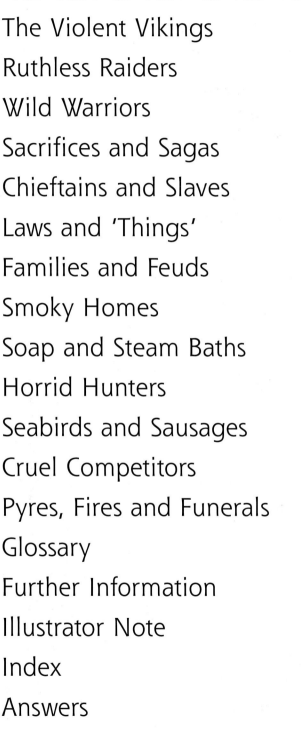

The Violent Vikings

▲ Vikings were feared warriors.

The Vikings lived over 1,000 years ago in the lands we now call Scandinavia. From around 800 CE, they were a feared and famous people. Although they were never united under one leader, they traded, **raided** and conquered for over 300 years.

They were great sailors, explorers, warriors and farmers. They built sleek, fast ships that travelled and traded as far as Europe, Africa, Asia and America.

They were master boat-builders and stone, wood and metal carvers. They were also skilled at farming, hunting and fishing.

▲ Viking helmets were made of iron

▲ The Vikings had their own alphabet of 16 letters called runes.

Viking Long Ships

Fierce monsters were carved on the **prows** of Viking longships. The Vikings believed they would scare off spirits protecting the lands they invaded. They could be removed when they sailed past friendly shores.

Gruesome truth

Those are some of the things that you probably already know about the Vikings, but in this book you'll find out the gory and grisly bits that no one ever tells you! Each double page will begin with a well-known FACT, before going on to tell you the **gruesome truth** about the Vikings. Look out for these features throughout the book – the answers are on page 32.

▼ Viking sailors used the position of the sun and the stars to navigate.

WHAT IS IT?
Guess the mystery object.

TRUE OR **FALSE?**
Decide if the statement is fact or fiction.

Ruthless Raiders

FACT The Vikings were great explorers, sailing to four continents to trade and conquer lands overseas.

Gruesome truth

Viking warriors **looted** treasures from churches and monasteries, seizing the priests and monks to kill or sell them as slaves.

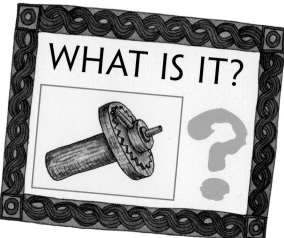

WHAT IS IT?

Sneaky ships

Viking raids began in the late 700s CE. The Vikings needed more land for farming because their population was growing and much of the countryside where they lived was hilly, forested or heathland. Their warships were sleek and fast. They could sail in just a metre of water, so they could sneak up rivers or be dragged onto beaches to launch surprise attacks. The largest longship could carry more than 60 rowers, along with horses and dozens of soldiers. Mice and rats also got on board and landed with the Vikings!

Boned to death

Viking raiders spread fear and panic. They demanded **ransoms** for **hostages** or money to leave people in peace. When they captured the Archbishop of Canterbury in 1011 CE and were refused a ransom to release him, they pelted him with cattle heads and bones before killing him with an axe.

▶ When the Viking Sigurd the Powerful killed an enemy leader in battle, he cut off his head and threw it over the saddle of his horse. But a tooth in the skull bit into his leg and he died from an infected wound.

In surprise attacks, Viking raiders burned buildings, stole belongings and seized prisoners.

Wild Warriors

FACT Viking warriors were fierce and skilled fighters. They had some of the best armour and weapons of their time.

Gruesome truth

Viking warriors fought vicious hand-to-hand fights using axes and daggers, and sometimes chopped off their captives' noses and hands.

Spears and swords

They fought with spears, axes, daggers and bows and arrows. There were two kinds of spear for throwing and thrusting and they had different shaped spearheads for fighting or hunting. Some spearsmen were so skilled they could throw two spears together using both hands, or catch an enemy spear and send it back.

Swords were their most treasured belongings. They gave them names like 'Leg biter' and 'Adder'. The blades were sharp on both sides and were up to 90 centimetres long.

▲ Viking weapons were treasured possessions and often had decorated handles or blades.

8

Whiffy wounds

When a warrior was wounded in battle, they fed him with onion porridge then smelt the wound. If they smelt onions, they knew he had been wounded right through to the stomach and would probably die!

▲ A smell of onions or leeks meant a wound could be fatal.

Berserkers

The most feared warriors were the Berserkers. They worshipped the god Odin and fought wearing bearskins because they believed it would lend them the animals' strength. They went into wild rages, rolling their eyes, frothing at the mouth and biting their shields. They may have been eating fly agaric, a type of poisonous toadstool, to send them into this rage. This is where the word 'berserk' comes from.

▲ If a fury came on them as they feasted, berserkers would rush out and wrestle with boulders until it wore off.

TRUE OR FALSE?
Viking warriors wore helmets with horns on.

Sacrifices and Sagas

FACT The Vikings worshipped **pagan** gods before their leaders became Christians. They passed their beliefs down the generations in long poems and stories called sagas.

Gruesome truth

The Vikings **sacrificed** people and animals to the gods. Human victims were stabbed or strangled, then sometimes 'blood-eagled'. This meant cutting down a man's back and opening out his rib cage and lungs like eagle wings. Dogs, horses, cattle and other animals were also sacrificed as offerings to please the gods.

▲ Human and animal heads were thrown into wells or rivers as offerings to the gods.

Violent tales

The Vikings enjoyed hearing violent and blood-thirsty sagas around the fireside. According to the sagas, gods like Odin, Thor and Frey were fierce and ruthless.

◄ Odin was the Viking god of war. They believed he rode a horse with eight legs and had only one eye because he had traded the other one in for a drink from the well of wisdom.

Giants and graffiti

The Vikings were a **superstitious** people who believed in evil giants, monsters, elves and gnomes. They wore lucky charms or **amulets** to protect them from harm.

Wherever they went, the Vikings left graffiti in letters called runes. They believed the runes had magic powers and used them for fortune-telling, spells and curses.

◀ Rune stones would have been brightly painted to catch the eye of passers by.

WHAT IS IT?

TRUE OR FALSE?
Thursday is named after the Viking god Thor.

▲ When a Viking made an animal sacrifice to the gods, he hung the carcass on poles outside his house to show off to his neighbours.

Chieftains and Slaves

FACT Viking kings were brave warriors who led their people in law and religion. They ruled over the chieftains who were landowners and warriors. Then came the freemen and under them the slaves, or **'thralls'**.

Gruesome truth

Kings had to have the support of their chieftains, because if they lost it they could be **exiled** or killed. The thralls had no rights at all. Their masters could beat them to death without penalty.

Muck and bones

Many slaves were people who had been captured during raids to sell on the slave markets. Some were freemen who had lost their land and money. Slaves had to have their master's permission to go anywhere or to get married. They did all the hard work in the house or on the land. A slave's job included picking through meat bones on rubbish heaps. Bones were used for everything from ice skates to whistles and needles.

▲ Slaves' jobs included digging out **peat** for fuel and spreading muck on farmland.

◀ Some slaves were monks captured during raids on monasteries.

WHAT IS IT?

Cruel kings

Viking kings who had become Christians sometimes killed or tortured people who refused to convert to Christianity. The punishments included poking out their eyes, cutting off their tongues and taking their sons as hostages.

▼ Slave traders sometimes exchanged a young boy slave for a goat or a fine rain cloak!

13

Law and 'Things'

FACT Viking laws were decided by 'The Things', assemblies of freemen who met together to discuss problems, settle arguments and punish crimes.

Gruesome truth

For the worst crimes like murder, a man could be outlawed by the Thing, which meant he lost his land and belongings, and anyone was free to kill him without punishment.

Criminals could also be made to pay fines to the families of men they had killed or injured. Thieves were punished by shaving and tarring their heads, then making them run between two lines of people who threw stones at them.

▼ Physical punishments included pelting the criminal with stones.

Oaths and ordeals

People accused of crimes could swear an **oath** to their innocence on a priest's holy ring, or go through an **ordeal** like walking over hot irons or putting their hands into a cauldron of boiling water to pick out hot stones. The Vikings believed that the gods would protect an innocent person from harm, and that if the wound healed quickly then the person was innocent.

▲ The Vikings believed if the accused was innocent the gods would heal their burns or wounds swiftly.

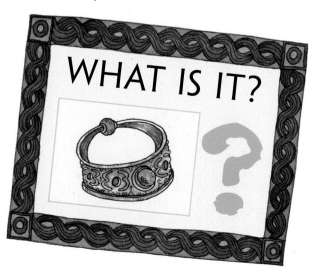

WHAT IS IT?

▲ The Thing also settled matters like divorce. A woman was free to divorce her husband for many 'crimes' like showing too much of his bare chest!

Families and Feuds

FACT Family was very important to the Vikings. They would fight anyone who insulted or harmed a family member.

Gruesome truth

Feuds between enemy families could last for generations. Houses were often burned down, dogs and horses killed and people murdered.

Fire and fury

Feuds could start with just a rude insult or a crime like stealing chickens. This sometimes led to revenge acts like dogs being strangled, horses poisoned and cows killed. Angry Vikings could set fire to their enemy's house and demand they come out and fight or die in the fire. If a Viking was murdered, it was the duty of his family to take revenge. Often they didn't kill the murderer but picked the most important member of his family instead.

▲ Money called 'wergild' (man value) had to be paid to the family of a man who had been murdered.

▲ Referees could order punishments by ordeal, such as grappling with a wild cow. The loser in a dispute had to wear greased shoes and hold onto a greased cow's tail. Another man whipped the cow, sending it into a wild frenzy. The man could save his life if he could hold on.

Deadly duels

If feuds went on for years, a referee from The Thing (see page 14) could be called in. He had to decide which family had suffered the most then order their enemies to pay them a fine. Sometimes he arranged for them to fight a duel called a holmganga. The rules were strict. If a man stepped off the cloak during the fight, he was declared a coward. At the end of the duel, the man with the most wounds had to pay his opponent in silver. If he was killed, the winner won all his property.

▲ The holmganga was a duel fought with weapons on a cloak, or animal hide, laid on the ground. Enemies fought until blood was spilled or only one man was left standing

Smoky Homes

FACT The Vikings lived in longhouses with a hearth in the middle for heating and cooking.

Gruesome truth

There was no chimney, just a smoke hole in the roof. The smell of smoke and gutted fish drying on racks mingled with the whiff of rubbish thrown onto the floor.

Muck and membranes

The only light in the house came from the fire or from smelly lamps that burned oil from whale blubber. There were no windows, just small openings in the walls covered with pigs' bladders or with the **membrane** from calves. The floors were made of earth covered with reeds or straw and animal muck was used to make the walls waterproof.

The fire was laid on a raised stone hearth in the middle of the house. If a baby died, a slave had the job of burying its body under the hearth.

▲ Fish was gutted and dried on racks to store through the winter months.

▶ Vikings shared part of the longhouse with animals during the winter months.

Wells and worms

Cattle or pigs lived in a separate room in the longhouse in winter and hens and geese roamed the streets feeding off the rubbish or '**midden**' heaps. Wells for water and **cess pits** for sewage were often side by side and the Vikings had gut worms from drinking dirty water. They used outside toilets that were usually just a pit dug in the ground with a wooden plank for a seat.

WHAT IS IT?

Soap and Steam Baths

FACT The Vikings kept themselves clean with steam baths. They made combs from antlers and soap from plants.

Gruesome truth

Bath houses were used once a week. Vikings poured hot water over stones to make the steam then beat themselves with twigs to get rid of the dirt and grime. In winter, they sometimes followed this with a roll in the snow!

▼ Steam baths were used to sweat away grime and dirt.

Conkers and cow dung

The Vikings made soap by peeling and mashing up conkers then mixing them with water and squeezing them out into a lump to dry. Sometimes they used nettles or wood ash instead. They had no toilet paper; they just used moss!

WHAT IS IT?

People stored their urine and soaked their clothes in it to clean them. The **ammonia** in urine helped to clean away dirt and oil.

▼ Viking men wore long hair and moustaches or beards. A wife's jobs included combing her husband's hair to get rid of nits and checking for fleas.

▲ Urine was used for soaking and cleaning clothes.

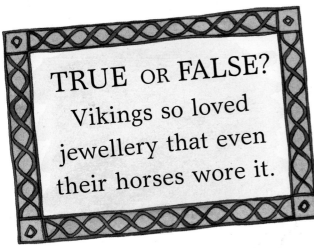

TRUE OR FALSE?
Vikings so loved jewellery that even their horses wore it.

Horrid Hunters

FACT The Vikings were skilled hunters and fishers.

Gruesome truth

Men climbed cliffs to steal sea birds' eggs and catch puffins and seagulls. They trapped them in nets at the end of long poles before wringing their necks.

◄ Around 12,000 puffins were caught each year. Puffins were roasted and seagulls were cooked in stews.

Teams of men in boats drove whales onto beaches in coastal bays, then speared, or **harpooned**, them to death. Walruses were killed for their tusks that were traded as ivory. The Vikings cut walrus skins in a long spiral from shoulder to tail to make them into strong ropes. They also captured or killed polar bears for their skins and meat which they sometimes ate raw.

▲ Walrus ivory was carved to make chess pieces and knife handles.

TRUE OR FALSE?
They used birds' foot bones as sewing needles.

Skis and spears

Vikings hunted every kind of animal, such as bears, boars and elks. They sometimes chased them on horseback or on skis and used spears and bows and arrows. Beavers, squirrels and foxes were trapped for their fur and they also **snared** ravens and other wild birds for food.

▼ Viking hunters were skilled riders.

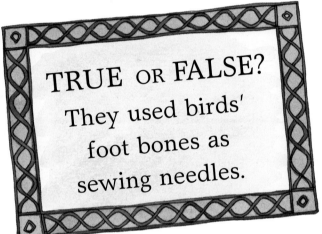

Seabirds and Sausages

FACT Viking women cooked bread, sausages and stews and salted, dried, pickled or smoked fish and meat to store through the winter months.

Gruesome truth

Vikings cooked baked seal, horse-meat kebabs and polar bear steaks. They also ate hare, boar, walrus, elk and whale.

▲ Vikings liked to eat seagull stew.

Bark bread

Wives or female slaves had the job of grinding the barley to make flour. If the barley harvest was poor, they made it from peas or pine tree bark. Viking bread was hard and gritty and wore away their teeth.

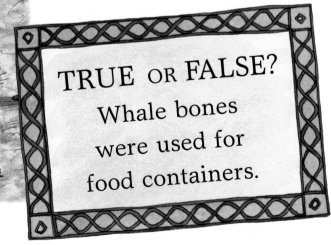

TRUE OR FALSE?
Whale bones were used for food containers.

▲ Bread often contained grit from the stone used for grinding flour.

Horse kebabs

At feasts, the meat was boiled or roasted but sometimes Viking men just warmed it inside their shirts and ate it raw! For important feasts, they sacrificed a horse to the gods and spit-roasted the horse-meat as kebabs. Horses were also killed for meat when they got old and worn out.

▼ For special feasts, Viking families invited their dead ancestors along by cleaning up their skull and bones and giving them a place at the table.

▲ Horse meat was roasted on sticks.

Horns and honey

Popular drinks were sour milk and **mead** made from honey. Vikings often got drunk on mead at feasts because they drank from hollow reindeer antlers or cowhorns that had to be emptied before they could be put down. Wedding feasts could last a whole month!

WHAT IS IT?

Cruel Competitors

FACT The Vikings enjoyed competitive sports like wrestling and swimming contests.

Gruesome truth

Swimmers sometimes tried to drown their rivals and wrestling matches could end in death.

Wrestlers and jugglers

The most widespread sport was wrestling. Some matches went on for hours and wrestlers used **cudgels**. People of all classes, including women, enjoyed wrestling. Water wrestling was also popular, with competitions taking place in nearby lakes and rivers.

▲ Sometimes competitors held their opponent's head under water until they gave up or drowned.

Other sports that tested strength and skill were fencing, archery, boulder-throwing and knife juggling.

▲ The Vikings practised dangerous skills like knife juggling.

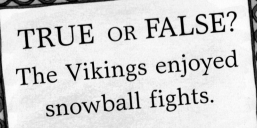

TRUE OR FALSE?
The Vikings enjoyed snowball fights.

Sparring stallions

Horse fighting was a popular spectator sport and people gambled on the winner. Stallions were trained to fight each other to the death.

▶ Male horses were trained to fight each other.

Fighting fit

Viking men used sport to keep them fit and prepare them for battle. In the summer, they held rowing races or carried out daring challenges like walking from oar to oar around a long ship whilst it was being rowed!

In the winter, they sometimes challenged each other to climb up a rock face or jump off a cliff. Even small boys practised sword play with wooden swords.

WHAT IS IT?

▲ Even the board game 'hnefatafl' could end in arguments and fights.

27

Pyres, Fires and Funerals

FACT The Vikings believed death was a journey to the next life. Funeral ceremonies for chieftains sometimes lasted several days.

Gruesome truth

The bodies of Viking chieftains were often burned in a ship with all their belongings, including dogs, horses and sometimes a favourite slave girl or wife.

The 'Angel of Death'

Kings, queens and chieftains were laid on cushions in a longship. A slave girl might volunteer, or be chosen, to die with her master. Mourners beat their shields with sticks to hide her screams while two men led her on board the ship and strangled her. Then an old woman called 'the Angel of Death' stabbed her with a dagger in the heart. The mourners set fire to the ship, sending the dead man or woman on their journey to the next life.

▶ Viking funerals took place by rivers, or near the coast, so that ships did not have to be dragged far over land. A relative of the dead man set fire to the ship and mourners joined in by throwing fire brands onto it.

▲ Viking women's grave goods included everything they needed for cooking and weaving.

Grave goods

Viking grave goods included everything that might be needed for the after life: food, beer, clothes, weapons and jewellery. The Vikings believed a ship would carry the dead safely on their journey and even simple graves were marked by stones in the shape of a ship. One Viking queen also took along a wagon, four sledges, two oxen, two tents and a camp bed for the journey!

► When a Viking died a long way from home, his friends sometimes asked monks to boil the body until just the bones were left so they could carry them home in a box.

 # Glossary

ammonia	A chemical solution that is used for cleaning.
amulets	Good luck charms worn to keep evil away.
cess pits	Pits for sewage.
cudgels	Thick sticks used as weapons.
duel	A fight between two people.
exiled	Sent away or banished.
feuds	Bitter fights between enemies.
harpooned	Stabbed with harpoons (sharp, barbed poles that are thrown).
hostages	People kidnapped and held captive.
looted	Robbed or stole.
mead	An alcoholic drink made from honey and water.
membrane	Stretchy skin tissue.
midden	A dump for kitchen and household waste.
navigate	Direct the course of a journey.
oath	A solemn promise.
ordeal	A trial or painful and difficult experience.
pagan	Believing in superstitions, spirits and gods.
peat	Organic matter dug out of marshland and used for fertiliser or fuel.
prows	The bows or fronts of ships or boats.
raided	Attacked and robbed.
ransoms	Sums demanded in exchange for hostages.
sacrificed	Killed as an offering.
snared	Caught with traps.
superstitious	Fearing and believing in things that are not based on scientific evidence
thralls	Slaves.
warriors	Soldiers.

Further Information

Books

100 Things You Should Know About the Vikings by Fiona MacDonald, Miles Kelly Publishing, 2005

Facts About the Vikings by Dereen Taylor, Wayland, 2007

History Relived: The Saxons and Vikings by Terry Deary and Martin Brown, Scholastic, 2007

How would you survive as a Viking? by Jacqueline Morley, Watts, 2005

The Vicious Vikings (Horrible Histories) by Terry Deary and Martin Brown, Scholastic, 2007

Websites

www.bbc.co.uk/schools/primary history/vikings
www.jorvik-viking-centre.co.uk
www.pbs.org/wgbh/nova/vikings

Places to visit

The British Museum, London
The Jorvik Viking Centre, York
The National Museum of Ireland, Dublin
The Viking Ship Museum, Oslo

Illustrator Note

When Matt was growing up he would have loved to have been a Viking, even if it was for one day. But after illustrating this book Matt has learnt that life for a Viking warrior wasn't all sea shanties and sailing. Life was in fact tough, hard and sometimes very gruesome indeed.

Matt Buckingham

Index

Answers

Page 6 What is it? A navigation table. An instrument that helped the Vikings navigate at sea.

Page 9 True or false? False. Most wore plain leather or iron helmets; only special ceremonial helmets may have been adorned with horns.

Page 11 What is it? A lucky amulet in the shape of the god Thor's hammer. Vikings believed that it was the hammer that made the sound of thunder.

Page 11 True or false? True.

Page 13 What is it? A lead weight. These weights were used with folding measuring scales by slave traders, and other traders.

Page 15 What is it? A priest's ring.

Page 19 What is it? A Viking toilet seat.

Page 21 What is it? Metal ear spoons for cleaning wax out of the ears.

Page 21 True or false? True. Vikings decorated their horses' bridles and harnesses with jewellery.

Page 23 True or false? True.

Page 24 True or false? True. They ate whale meat and used the blubber to make oil for fuel.

Page 25 What is it? A reindeer horn used for drinking.

Page 26 True or false? True. They also skied, skated and sledged in the winter months.

Page 27 What is it? A Viking skate made from a cow- or horse-foot bone.